I0410868

September 2014

PATIENT PROTECTION AND AFFORDABLE CARE ACT

Procedures for Reporting Certain Financial Management Information Should Be Improved

PATIENT PROTECTION AND AFFORDABLE CARE ACT

Procedures for Reporting Certain Financial Management Information Should Be Improved

GAO Highlights

Highlights of GAO-14-697, a report to congressional requesters

Why GAO Did This Study

PPACA makes significant changes in the way health insurance in the United States is provided, including changes to private health insurance coverage. GAO was asked to examine the resources that CCIIO used and expects to use in implementing the private health insurance provisions of PPACA. GAO's objective was to identify resources that CCIIO received, used, and expects to use from enactment of PPACA through fiscal year 2014, including certain categories of expenditures, the sources of funding, and the total number of staff, along with the number of staff reassigned from other units.

To perform this work GAO obtained the information requested and compared it to available supporting documentation, reviewed available related policies and procedures, and interviewed CMS officials.

What GAO Recommends

GAO recommends that CMS identify and evaluate options to facilitate reporting CCIIO-related financial management information that is independently verifiable in a timely manner, and develop and implement policies and procedures to document the preparation, review, and approval of information produced for nonroutine requests.

HHS did not concur with GAO's recommendations. In its view, CMS's existing procedures are adequate to respond to nonroutine information requests. However, as discussed in this report, GAO continues to believe that enhancements to CMS's procedures are needed and that the recommendations are valid.

View GAO-14-697. For more information, contact Beryl H. Davis at (202) 512-2623 or davisbh@gao.gov.

What GAO Found

The Department of Health and Human Service's (HHS) Centers for Medicare and Medicaid Services (CMS) provided GAO with most of the requested data regarding financial resources that the Center for Consumer Information and Insurance Oversight (CCIIO) and other CMS offices received, used, and expect to use to implement the private health insurance and health insurance exchange provisions of the Patient Protection and Affordable Care Act (PPACA) for which CCIIO is responsible from its enactment in March 2010 through fiscal year 2014. However, CMS did not provide estimates of fiscal year 2014 obligations for certain categories of CCIIO-related transactions, such as advertising and other public relations activities. In addition, CMS provided data on CCIIO's staffing levels as of September 30, 2013, but did not provide complete staffing reassignment data.

GAO was unable to consistently verify the reliability of the data received from CMS. Specifically:

- GAO was able to determine the reliability of CMS's estimates for total obligations for fiscal year 2014, which was $3.7 billion; the number of staff as of September 30, 2013, which was 347; and total salary expenditures from March 2010 through fiscal year 2013, which were $79.8 million.
- GAO could not determine the reliability of any of the other financial information CMS provided because CMS's core financial system did not produce totals for much of the CCIIO-related information requested. For example, the system did not produce expenditure totals for CCIIO-related polling, focus groups, or advertising and other public relations activities because of how these activities are captured in the system. Similarly, information related to reassignment of staff to CCIIO from other CMS and HHS units was not readily available. Consequently, the staff reassignment information provided to GAO was not complete, was not supported by documentary evidence, and could not be verified.

GAO identified several issues that contributed to CMS's inability to provide complete information that is independently verifiable in a timely manner. First, CMS does not have an effective means of identifying CCIIO-related information. While CMS had policies and procedures for its standard financial operations, it did not have documented policies and procedures for responding to nonroutine information requests. Instead, CMS relied on ad hoc manual procedures that were labor intensive and time consuming. As a result, CMS required an extended period of time to provide most of the information GAO requested, in some cases taking several months. Second, CMS does not have documented procedures to ensure that data requests are reviewed and approved for accuracy. CMS officials told GAO that the information they provided had been subject to review and approval at several levels, including review by subject matter experts. However, these procedures were not documented. Consequently, GAO was not able to independently verify that they had been properly performed. Because CMS's processes are inconsistent with certain federal accounting and internal control standards, Congress and other decision makers may not have access to timely and reliable CCIIO-related information that they may need to make resource allocation decisions and assessments of program performance.

_____ United States Government Accountability Office

Contents

September 22, 2014

The Honorable Dave Camp
Chairman
Committee on Ways and Means
House of Representatives

The Honorable Charles Boustany
Chairman
Subcommittee on Oversight
Committee on Ways and Means
House of Representatives

The Patient Protection and Affordable Care Act (PPACA),[1] which was enacted in March 2010, includes provisions to expand access to public and private health insurance—including through the creation of health insurance exchanges—and made a number of changes affecting the provision of private health insurance.[2] Responsibility for implementation of the act's provisions regarding private health insurance and establishment of health insurance exchanges was originally assigned by the Secretary of Health and Human Services to the Office of Consumer Information and Insurance Oversight (OCIIO), within the Office of the Secretary, under the Department of Health and Human Services (HHS). In January 2011, this responsibility was transferred by the Secretary to HHS's Centers for Medicare and Medicaid Services (CMS), which created a new office, the Center for Consumer Information and Insurance

---

[1]Pub. L. No. 111-148 (Mar. 23, 2010), *as amended by* the Health Care and Education Reconciliation Act of 2010 (HCERA), Pub. L. No. 111-152 (Mar. 30, 2010). In this report, references to PPACA include any amendments made by HCERA.

[2]Health insurance exchanges are marketplaces where eligible individuals may compare and select among insurance plans offered by participating private issuers of health coverage. PPACA directed states to establish state-based exchanges by January 1, 2014. In states electing not to establish and operate such exchanges, PPACA requires the federal government to establish and operate exchanges in the states, referred to as the federally facilitated exchanges.

Oversight (CCIIO), to assume the responsibility, and OCIIO was disestablished.[3]

You asked us to examine the financial and staff resources used or expected to be used by CMS in implementing the private health insurance provisions of PPACA from its enactment through fiscal year 2014. Our objective was to identify the CCIIO-related resources that CMS received, used, and expects to use to implement PPACA from enactment though fiscal year 2014, including certain categories of expenditures; the source of the funding; the number of CCIIO staff and CMS staff working on CCIIO-related activities as of September 30, 2013; and the number of staff reassigned from other units.

To achieve our objective, we contacted responsible officials at CMS to request information on (1) data concerning total CCIIO-related obligations[4] and expenditures from the enactment of PPACA in March 2010 through fiscal year 2013,[5] including amounts related to salaries, travel, advertising and other public relations activities, polling and focus groups, and conferences; (2) CMS's estimates of obligations in total and in each of these categories for fiscal year 2014; and (3) the number of full- and part-time CCIIO staff as of September 30, 2013, including the number reassigned from other CMS and HHS units. We also requested available supporting documentation for the information provided to assist in determining its reliability and reviewed policies and procedures and internal controls in place intended to help to ensure the reliability of the

---

[3]CMS created CCIIO to oversee the implementation of the PPACA provisions related to private health insurance and health insurance exchanges. While CCIIO is the primary office responsible for implementation, other CMS offices and centers also perform services in support of the implementation of these provisions, and the related amounts are included in this report. In this report, "CCIIO-related" refers to all CMS obligations and expenditures for implementing PPACA's private health insurance and exchange provisions.

[4]Obligations are legal liabilities of an agency to pay for goods and services ordered or received. An agency incurs an obligation, for example, when it places an order, signs a contract, awards a grant, purchases a service, or takes other actions that require the government to make payments to the public or from one government account to another. Expenditures are the actual spending of money through the issuance of checks, disbursement of cash, or electronic transfer of funds made to liquidate an obligation.

[5]Prior to the establishment of CCIIO within CMS, OCIIO obligations and expenditures were recorded in the Unified Financial Management System within the Office of the Secretary.

information and to assess its applicability to our audit objectives and conformance with *Standards for Internal Control in the Federal Government.*[6] In order to determine whether the information provided was reliable,[7] we also analyzed the information we received, conducted follow-up inquiries with agency officials to ensure that we had received what we requested, and compared the information to available supporting documentation. As discussed in the report, we were not able to determine the reliability of most of the information. In addition, we met with officials from the Office of Inspector General of HHS and the independent auditor of the fiscal year 2013 and 2012 CMS financial statements to determine whether they were aware of any issues pertinent to our objectives that we should consider in designing our audit procedures. For further details of our scope and methodology, see appendix I.

We conducted this performance audit from January 2013 to September 2014 in accordance with generally accepted government auditing standards. Those standards require that we plan and perform the audit to obtain sufficient, appropriate evidence to provide a reasonable basis for our findings and conclusions based on our audit objectives. We believe that the evidence obtained provides a reasonable basis for our findings and conclusions based on our audit objectives.

Background

HHS is one of several federal agencies collectively responsible for implementing the provisions of PPACA related to private health insurance and health insurance exchanges.[8] Within HHS, CMS is the primary component responsible for PPACA implementation. In 2011, CMS created CCIIO, one of six centers under CMS, to oversee implementation of PPACA's private health insurance and health insurance exchange

---

[6]GAO, *Standards for Internal Control in the Federal Government*, GAO/AIMD-00-21.3.1. (Washington, D.C.: November 1999).

[7]For financial information to be considered reliable, it must be determined to be (1) complete (includes all applicable information), (2) accurate (free of material error or fraud), and (3) valid (includes only financial information that accurately represents the substance of the nature of the underlying financial activity).

[8]Other federal agencies involved in the implementation of the private health insurance provisions of PPACA include the Employee Benefits Security Administration under the Department of Labor and the Internal Revenue Service under the Department of the Treasury.

provisions.[9] PPACA provided much of the funding used by CMS to implement the CCIIO-related private health insurance and health insurance exchange provisions it contains.[10] Most such funding provided by PPACA is dedicated to funding these CCIIO-related provisions and cannot be used for any other CMS activities.[11] However, CMS also used funding provided by other legislation that was not specifically dedicated to the private health insurance and health insurance exchange provisions of PPACA and thus was also available to fund other CMS activities. This includes CMS's annual Program Management appropriation, which provides funding for CMS's administrative activities and the Health Insurance Reform Implementation Fund.[12] Funding for CCIIO-related activities represents a relatively small portion of the total funding used by CMS and recorded in its core financial system, the Healthcare Integrated General Ledger Accounting System (HIGLAS). For example, for fiscal year 2013, CMS reported that it incurred obligations totaling $1.16 trillion of which $5.72 billion (0.49 percent) was for CCIIO-related transactions according to data provided by CMS.[13]

---

[9]In addition, CMS has 15 operational offices responsible for other functions, including aspects of the Medicare and Medicaid programs.

[10]PPACA provided appropriations for implementation of the Consumer Assistance Program ($30 million), Rate Reviews ($250 million), Pre-Existing Condition Insurance Plan (PCIP) ($5 billion), Employee Retirement Reinsurance Plan ($5 billion), Consumer Operated and Oriented Plan ($6 billion, $3.9 billion of which was subsequently rescinded), and Affordable Insurance Exchange Grants (an indefinite amount to be determined annually by the Secretary of HHS). For exchanges being operated directly by the federal government, the user fees paid by issuers participating in the exchanges are also included in CMS's CCIIO-related funding. In addition, as allowed under the PPACA PCIP provision, CMS also collects premiums from PCIP enrollees that CMS uses to fund the cost of the program.

[11]CMS has also drawn on appropriations provided under PPACA for the Prevention and Public Health Fund for other CMS activities. From enactment through fiscal year 2013, these accounted for about 2.6 percent of total appropriated funds obligated by CMS for PPACA CCIIO-related purposes. All other CCIIO-related appropriations provided under PPACA were dedicated to CCIIO-related activities only.

[12]The Health Insurance Reform Implementation Fund was established by section 1005 of the Health Care and Education Reconciliation Act of 2010, Pub. L. No. 111-152 (Mar. 30, 2010), appropriating $1 billion to HHS for federal administrative expenses to carry out both that act and PPACA.

[13]CMS's obligations incurred include amounts related to the Medicare and Medicaid programs.

CMS's accounting for CCIIO-related transactions is significantly affected by the manner in which transactions are funded and recorded in HIGLAS, which is used by all of CMS's 21 offices and centers, including CCIIO. Appropriated funds are recorded in HIGLAS using separate appropriation accounts established by the Department of the Treasury (Treasury).[14] Each year, CMS uses funding from these appropriation accounts to support its activities, including the implementation of the CCIIO-related private health insurance provisions of PPACA. HIGLAS accounts for financial transactions by appropriation account to ensure that funds are obligated and expended in accordance with applicable appropriations law. Accordingly, the appropriation accounts in HIGLAS correspond to the related budgetary funding sources that gave rise to them, rather than to the CMS office responsible for implementing the specific activities for which the funding was provided. Consequently, appropriation accounts that were created based on legislation that funds only CCIIO-related activities will include only CCIIO-related transactions, and appropriation accounts that were created based on legislation that funds both CCIIO-related and non-CCIIO-related CMS activities will include both types of transactions.

Each fiscal year from 2010 through 2013, CMS's financial statements, which were derived from its core financial system, were audited by an independent public accountant (IPA). In each of these years, the IPA concluded that CMS's financial balance sheets—and statements of net costs, changes in net position, and budgetary resources—were free of material misstatement.[15] This provides assurance that totals produced by HIGLAS constitute reliable evidence of the nature of the underlying transactions and their total dollar amount.

---

[14]Treasury appropriation accounts are assigned by Treasury, in collaboration with the Office of Management and Budget (OMB) and the affected agency, to each individual appropriation, receipt, or other fund account. Financial transactions of the federal government are classified by appropriation account for reporting to Treasury and OMB.

[15]Because of significant uncertainties primarily related to the achievement of the projected reductions in Medicare cost growth reflected in the fiscal years 2010, 2011, 2012, and 2013 Statements of Social Insurance and Statements of Changes in Social Insurance Amounts, CMS's independent auditor was unable to express an opinion on these financial statements. However, these issues did not affect CCIIO-related transactions or the integrity of HIGLAS totals.

Limitations in CMS's Policies and Procedures Impeded Efforts to Determine the Reliability of Most of the CCIIO-Related Resources That CMS Reported It Received and Used

CMS provided most of the CCIIO-related information we requested, but limitations in its policies and procedures made the process of obtaining it difficult and time consuming, and we could not determine the reliability of most of the amounts CMS provided. For several reasons, CMS's core financial system—HIGLAS—did not produce CCIIO-specific totals for much of the financial information we requested, and CMS did not have an efficient alternate approach for identifying the information. Expenditure totals for certain activities—for example, advertising—could not be distinguished from other transactions because CMS had not assigned identifying codes to identify the CMS office or the nature of the activity in HIGLAS. Also, HIGLAS does not produce totals of CCIIO-related travel and salary transactions in total or by funding source. In addition, information regarding staff reassignments to CCIIO from other CMS and HHS units was not readily available, and the related information CMS provided was incomplete and not supported by documentary evidence. CMS did not have policies and procedures for responding to nonroutine information requests such as ours. Consequently, CMS employed an ad hoc manual process to identify the information requested, which was labor intensive and time consuming. In addition, CMS's procedures for identifying and obtaining the information and its review and approval were not documented, so we also could not verify that these procedures had been properly performed.

Statement of Federal Financial Accounting Standards No. 4, *Managerial Cost Accounting Standards and Concepts*,[16] and Statement of Federal Financial Accounting Concepts No.1, *Objectives of Federal Financial Reporting*,[17] highlight the importance of reliable and timely information to key stakeholders, such as managers, executives, and Congress, to support informed resource allocation decisions and assessments of program performance and the need for it to be verifiable. In addition, *Standards for Internal Control in the Federal Government* requires that internal control be clearly documented and that the documentation be readily available for examination.[18] Because CMS was not able to provide

---

[16]Federal Accounting Standards Advisory Board, *Statement of Federal Financial Accounting Standards No. 4: Managerial Cost Accounting Standards and Concepts*, (Washington, D.C.: July 31, 1995).

[17]Federal Accounting Standards Advisory Board, *Statement of Federal Financial Accounting Concepts No. 1: Objectives of Federal Financial Reporting*, (Washington, D.C.: Sept. 2, 1993).

[18]GAO/AIMD-00-21.3.1.

timely CCIIO-related information whose reliability could be independently determined, Congress and other decision makers may not have timely and reliable CCIIO-related financial management information, which could hamper efforts to make informed resource allocation decisions and assessment of program performance.

CMS Provided Most of the Requested Information

CMS provided most of the CCIIO-related financial management information we requested, which consisted of (1) total CCIIO-related obligations and expenditures from the enactment of PPACA through fiscal year 2013; (2) estimates of total CCIIO-related obligations for expenditures for fiscal year 2014; (3) the number of full-time CCIIO staff as of September 30, 2013;[19] and (4) total CCIIO-related expenditures from the enactment of PPACA through fiscal year 2013 for salaries, travel, advertising and other public relations activities, polling and focus groups, and conferences. However, CMS did not provide complete information regarding the following:

- Estimates of fiscal year 2014 CCIIO-related obligations (1) for staff salaries funded by legislation that also funds salaries related to other non-CCIIO related CMS activities or (2) related to the Prevention and Public Health Fund, travel, advertising and other public relations activities, polling and focus groups, and conferences. CMS did not provide estimates of fiscal year 2014 obligations for these specific categories because it did not prepare related estimates at this level of detail.

- Reassignments of staff to CCIIO from Medicare, Medicaid, or other CMS or HHS divisions and offices. CMS did not provide complete staff reassignment information because according to CMS officials, obtaining it would require review of each staff member's personnel file, which would be labor intensive and time consuming.

As discussed in the following section, although CMS was able to provide most of the information we requested, the reliability of most of it could not be determined.

---

[19]CMS informed us it did not have any CCIIO staff who were working only part-time.

Reliability of Most of the Information CMS Provided Could Not Be Determined

Because of limitations in CMS's policies and procedures, we could not determine the reliability of most of the CCIIO-related financial management information that CMS provided. Specifically, CMS did not record and retain the information in a manner that facilitated its retrieval in a form that lent itself to independent verification of reliability. CMS extracted most of the requested data from HIGLAS based on transaction codes and provided it to us on manually prepared spreadsheets. However, CMS's core financial system—HIGLAS, which is the basis of its audited financial statements—did not produce corresponding totals. As a result, there were no HIGLAS totals to which the CMS-provided spreadsheet amounts could be compared for purposes of determining whether they included all appropriate data that were contained in HIGLAS and could therefore be considered complete. Also, certain expenditures had not been assigned identifying transaction codes in HIGLAS, so the system was unable to produce related totals. In addition, the staff reassignment information provided by CMS was not supported by documentary evidence and therefore its reliability could also not be determined.

Some of the Information CMS Provided Was Determined to Be Reliable

We determined that CMS's estimates of total obligations for expenditures for fiscal year 2014—both in total and by funding source—were reliable. Also, estimates of salary expenditures funded by appropriation accounts that fund only CCIIO-related activities were reliable. To make these determinations, we reconciled CMS's estimates to the President's Budget and reviewed the logic underlying subsequent updates to the estimates, which we determined to be reasonable. These data, which we determined to be reliable, are shown in table 1.

Table 1: Reliability Could Be Determined for Center for Consumer Information and Insurance Oversight (CCIIO) Related Estimated Total Obligations and Salary Obligations, Fiscal Year 2014

Dollars in thousands

Funding source	Total estimated obligations for FY 2014[a]	Estimated staff salary obligations for FY 2014[b]
Amounts funded by appropriation accounts that fund only CCIIO-related activities		
Consumer Assistance Program Grants	$0	$0
Grants to states for premium review	0	N/A
Pre-Existing Condition Insurance Plan	358,134	5,000
Early Retiree Reinsurance Program	8,140	1,000
Affordable Insurance Exchanges Grants to States	1,342,521	8,000
Consumer Operated and Oriented Plan Program Account	16,900	5,000
Exchange user fees	200,000	0
Subtotal	**$1,925,695**	**$19,000**
Amounts funded by appropriation accounts that fund CCIIO-related and non-CCIIO related activities		
Health Insurance Reform Implementation Fund	$20,000	N/P
Department of Health and Human Services general departmental management	0	N/P
Program Management	1,326,302	N/P
Secretary's transfer authority	109,432	N/P
Nonrecurring Expenses Fund	352,982	N/P
Prevention and Public Health Fund	0	N/P
Subtotal	**$1,808,716**	**N/P**
Grand total for all funding sources	**$3,734,411**	**N/P**

Source: GAO analysis of Centers for Medicare and Medicaid Services data. | GAO-14-697

Legend: FY = fiscal year; N/A = not applicable; N/P = none prepared.

[a]According to the Centers for Medicare and Medicaid Services (CMS), these amounts represent CMS's most recent estimates of total obligations for fiscal year 2014 as of June 30, 2014.

[b]The fiscal year 2014 salary obligations estimates were reported in the CMS President's Budget as of April 10, 2013. CMS developed estimates of staff salaries for each funding source using an HHS-wide methodology. CMS prepares estimates of staff salaries for funding sources that are used exclusively for private health insurance and health insurance exchange activities and are attributable to CCIIO. However, for the appropriation accounts that are used for private health insurance and health insurance exchange activities as well as other activities, CMS did not prepare separate estimates of salary expenditures. Salary expenditure estimates are also included in the related CMS's budget request amounts for fiscal year 2014.

In addition, data provided by CMS on the total CCIIO salary expenditures from March 2010 through September 30, 2013, which was $79.8 million, as well as the related number of full-time CCIIO staff as of September 30, 2013, which was 347, were determined to be reliable.[20] To make this determination, we estimated total CCIIO salary expenditures based on the number of full-time staff assigned to CCIIO over this period and their salary levels, compared our estimate to the total CCIIO salary expenditures provided by CMS, and found the difference to be reasonable.

Reliability Could Not Be Determined for CCIIO-Related Amounts Partially Funded by Appropriation Accounts That Also Fund Non-CCIIO Activities

Because CMS's core financial system (HIGLAS) does not produce totals for a portion of the CCIIO-related obligations and expenditures in total or by their funding sources, we could not determine whether these amounts were complete, which is a major factor in determining reliability. A portion of CCIIO-related expenditures are funded from appropriation accounts that also fund non-CCIIO related CMS activities and therefore include both CCIIO-related and non-CCIIO-related CMS transactions. In such cases, HIGLAS does not produce CCIIO-related totals for these obligations and expenditures. Consequently, there were no CCIIO-related totals produced by HIGLAS to which we could compare the amounts provided by CMS for the purpose of determining their completeness. Information provided by CMS indicated that from PPACA's enactment through September 30, 2013, a total of $2.1 billion in CCIIO-related obligations and $714 million of CCIIO-related expenditures were included in appropriation accounts that also funded CMS activities unrelated to CCIIO, as detailed in table 2. However, because we were unable to determine whether these amounts were complete, we do not have any assurance whether these amounts are reliable and whether the actual amounts are larger.

[20]As discussed later and shown in table 3, we could not determine whether salary expenditure amounts by funding source were reliable.

Table 2: Reliability Could Not Be Determined for Center for Consumer Information and Insurance Oversight (CCIIO) Related Total Obligations and Expenditures, March 2010 through Fiscal Year 2013

Dollars in millions

Funding source	Total obligations March 2010 through FY 2013[a]	Total expenditures March 2010 through FY 2013
Amounts funded by appropriation accounts that fund only CCIIO-related activities[b]		
Consumer Assistance Program Grants	$28	$25
Grants to states for premium review	221	54
Pre-Existing Condition Insurance Plan	4,971	4,744
Early Retiree Reinsurance Program	4,980	4,961
Affordable Insurance Exchanges Grants to States	4,171	881
Consumer Operated and Oriented Plan Program Account	873	319
Exchange user fees	N/A	N/A
Subtotal	**$15,244**	**$10,984**
Amounts funded by appropriation accounts that fund CCIIO-related and non-CCIIO related activities		
Health Insurance Reform Implementation Fund	$314	$162
Department of Health and Human Services general departmental management	98	92
Program Management	771	393
Secretary's transfer authority	114	2
Nonrecurring Expenses Fund	300	63
Prevention and Public Health Fund	454	2
Subtotal	**$2,051**	**$714**
Grand total for all funding sources	**$17,295**	**$11,698**

Source: GAO analysis of Centers for Medicare and Medicaid Services data. | GAO-14-697

Legend: FY = fiscal year; N/A = not applicable.

[a]These amounts reflect the total of obligations incurred during fiscal years 2010, 2011, 2012, and 2013, whether they are still outstanding or have been liquidated.

[b]Because these amounts are funded by appropriation accounts that fund only CCIIO-related activities, the Healthcare Integrated General Ledger Accounting System (HIGLAS) produces related totals, and we were able to determine that they are complete. However, the grand totals into which they are accumulated also include activity funded by appropriation accounts that fund both CCIIO-related and non-CCIIO related activities for which HIGLAS does not produce totals. As a result, we could not verify the completeness of the grand totals for all funding sources.

Reliability Could Not Be Determined for CCIIO-Related Salary or Travel Expenditures by Funding Source or for Travel Expenditures in Total

Because HIGLAS does not produce totals of CCIIO-related salary or travel expenditures, we also could not determine whether the amounts that CMS provided for CCIIO-related salary or travel expenditures by funding source, or travel expenditures in total, were reliable. CMS officials provided salary and travel expenditure amounts that they had extracted from HIGLAS and placed on manually prepared spreadsheets. However, there were no HIGLAS totals for salary or travel expenditures to which we could compare the related amounts provided by CMS to determine if they were complete, as detailed in table 3. As noted above, total salary expenditures of $79.8 million from March 2010 through fiscal year 2013 were determined to be reliable.

Table 3: Reliability Could Not Be Determined for Center for Consumer Information and Insurance Oversight (CCIIO) Related Salary and Travel Expenditures by Funding Source and Travel Expenditures in Total, March 2010 through Fiscal Year 2013

Dollars in thousands

Funding source	Salary expenditures from March 2010 through FY 2013	Travel expenditures from March 2010 through FY 2013
Amounts funded by appropriation accounts that fund only CCIIO-related activities		
Consumer Assistance Program Grants	$416	$3
Grants to states for premium review	0	0
Pre-Existing Condition Insurance Plan Program	4,588	150
Early Retiree Reinsurance Program	1,836	9
Affordable Insurance Exchanges Grants to States	12,055	308
Consumer Operated and Oriented Plan Program Account	2,467	33
Exchange user fees	0	0
Subtotal	**$21,362**	**$503**
Amounts funded by appropriation accounts that fund CCIIO-related and non-CCIIO related activities		
Health Insurance Reform Implementation Fund	$11,494	$245
Department of Health and Human Services general departmental management	8,900	49
Program Management	38,087	259
Secretary's transfer authority	0	0
Nonrecurring Expenses Fund	0	0
Prevention and Public Health Fund	0	0
Subtotal	**$58,481**	**$553**
Grand total for all funding sources	**$79,843**[a]	**$1,056**

Source: GAO analysis of Centers for Medicare and Medicaid Services data. | GAO-14-697

Legend: FY = fiscal year; N/A = not applicable.

[a]We determined that total salary expenditures provided by the Centers for Medicare and Medicaid Services (CMS) were reliable based on analytical comparison of the amount provided by CMS with related salary levels of individual CCIIO staff members, rather than Healthcare Integrated General Ledger Accounting System information. However, we could not determine the reliability of the underlying subtotals by funding source.

Reliability Could Not Be Determined for Expenditures for Advertising and Other Public Relations Activities, Polling and Focus Groups, and Conferences

HIGLAS does not produce totals of CCIIO-related expenditures for advertising and other public relations activities, polling and focus groups, and conferences because CMS has not assigned these activities identifying transaction codes that identify the nature of the activity and the related CMS office so that they can be separately identified and tracked in HIGLAS. Consequently, HIGLAS cannot distinguish them from other transactions or produce related totals. Also, because there are no codes identifying these types of transactions, CMS staff could not identify them in HIGLAS as being CCIIO-related transactions and extract them as they had with the CCIIO-related portions of total obligations, total expenditures, salaries, and travel expenditures. Instead, CMS staff identified these expenditures by manually reviewing individual underlying contracts. Because HIGLAS does not produce totals for these CCIIO-related expenditures to which we could compare CMS-provided amounts for purposes of determining their completeness, we could not determine their reliability, as detailed in table 4.

Table 4: Reliability Could Not Be Determined for Center for Consumer Information and Insurance Oversight (CCIIO) Related Expenditures for Advertising and Other Public Relations Activities, Polling and Focus Groups, and Conferences, March 2010 through Fiscal Year 2013

Dollars in thousands

Funding source	Advertising and other public relations activities Expenditures	Polling and focus groups Expenditures	Conferences Expenditures
Amounts funded by appropriation accounts that fund only CCIIO-related activities			
Consumer Assistance Program Grants	$0	$0	$0
Grants to states for premium review	0	0	0
Pre-Existing Condition Insurance Plan Program	309	0	0
Early Retiree Reinsurance Program	0	0	0
Affordable Insurance Exchanges Grants to States	0	0	166
Consumer Operated and Oriented Plan program account	0	0	164
Exchange user fees	0	0	0
Subtotal	**$309**	**$0**	**$330**
Amounts funded by appropriation accounts that fund CCIIO-related and non-CCIIO related activities			
Health Insurance Reform Implementation Fund	$0	$2,432	$368
Department of Health and Human Services general departmental management	0	0	0
Program Management	22,291	1,707	3,635
Secretary's transfer authority	0	0	0
Nonrecurring Expenses Fund	0	0	0
Prevention and Public Health Fund	255	0	0
Subtotal	**$22,546**	**$4,139**	**$4,003**
Grand total for all funding sources	**$22,855**	**$4,139**	**$4,333**

Source: GAO analysis of Centers for Medicare and Medicaid Services data. | GAO-14-697

Reliability Could Not Be Determined for Reassignment of Staff Information

The information CMS provided regarding reassignment of staff to CCIIO from other CMS or other HHS offices was not complete and was based on personal recollection unsupported by documentary evidence, as previously discussed. Consequently, we could not determine if it was reliable. CMS officials indicated that this information was not readily available and obtaining it would have required labor-intensive and time-consuming review of each staff member's individual personnel file. Of the 347 full-time CCIIO staff as of September 30, 2013, CMS provided information based on personal recollection that indicated that 92 staff had been reassigned from other CMS or HHS offices, including 5 who had been reassigned from the Medicare or Medicaid programs. CMS also informed us that 24 staff were assigned to CCIIO on temporary detail from other CMS or HHS offices as of September 30, 2013. According to CMS officials, 4 of these staff were detailed from the Medicare program, and 8 were detailed from offices that support the Medicare and Medicaid programs. However, we could not determine if these data were reliable. CMS did not provide any information regarding the previous assignments of the 255 other full-time CCIIO staff as of September 30, 2013.

CMS Did Not Have Adequate Policies and Procedures for Identifying CCIIO-Related Financial Management Information

CMS officials informed us that although they have established policies and procedures governing CMS's standard financial operations, they do not have established policies and procedures for responding to nonroutine information requests, such as those that might originate from Congress or other oversight bodies. Instead, CMS used ad hoc, largely manual procedures that consisted of either extracting CCIIO-related transactions from HIGLAS using transaction codes to identify them as CCIIO related or, for certain categories of expenditures that did not have such codes, manually reviewing underlying individual contracts. CMS used similar manual transaction identification and extraction procedures to produce its quarterly Status of Funds Report, which reflects CCIIO-related obligations and expenditure information that CMS management routinely uses to help support CCIIO-related budgetary and spending decisions. CMS officials informed us that HIGLAS possesses a "query" feature enabling users to produce custom reports to meet information needs not covered by existing standard reports. However, they also indicated that in part because of competing demands and resource constraints, they had been unable to develop and employ this functionality.

The largely manual, ad hoc process CMS employed was labor intensive and time consuming, and it often required an extended period of time to respond to our requests, in some cases several months. For example:

- In March 2013, we requested information regarding expenditures related to polling and focus groups, advertising and other public relations, and conferences. CMS did not provide us this information until about a year later, in March 2014.

- In March 2013, we requested a listing of CCIIO employees who had been reassigned to CCIIO from other HHS or CMS offices when CCIIO was created in 2011 and the offices from which they had been reassigned. However, CMS did not provide this information until about 4 months later, in July 2013. As discussed above, this information was not complete.

Statement of Federal Financial Accounting Concepts No. 1, *Objectives of Federal Financial Reporting,*[21] recognizes that if financial reports are to be useful, they must be issued soon enough to affect decisions, and that the passage of time usually diminishes the usefulness that the information otherwise would have had. Statement of Federal Financial Accounting Standards No. 4, *Managerial Cost Accounting Standards and Concepts,*[22] observes that cost information that is timely as well as reliable helps government managers ensure that resources are spent to achieve expected results and outputs and alerts them to waste and inefficiency. This concept also applies to other forms of financial management information. *Standards for Internal Control in the Federal Government* also recognizes that information should be recorded and communicated to management and others in a form and within a time frame that enables them to carry out their internal control and other responsibilities.[23]

We also found that CMS also did not have policies and procedures that required documented review and approval of the information provided in response to nonroutine requests to help ensure the reliability of financial management information. Although CMS officials informed us that the CCIIO-related financial management information we were provided was subject to multiple levels of review and approval before we received it, including review by subject matter experts, its review and approval of the CCIIO-related information provided to us were not documented. Consequently, we were unable to independently verify that these reviews and approvals had taken place. Our concern also applies to CMS's Status of Funds Report, which is a standard quarterly report that CMS uses to assist in making budgetary and spending decisions. According to CMS, this report was also prepared using a similar largely manual process, and review and approval of this report were also not documented. Such reviews and approvals are important internal control activities that can help provide reasonable assurance that information is reliable.

Standards for Internal Control in the Federal Government requires that internal control be clearly documented and that the documentation be

---

[21]Federal Accounting Standards Advisory Board, *Statement of Federal Financial Accounting Concepts No. 1, Objectives of Federal Financial Reporting.*

[22]Federal Accounting Standards Advisory Board, *Statement of Federal Financial Accounting Standards No. 4, Managerial Cost Accounting Standards and Concepts.*

[23]GAO/AIMD-00-21.3.1.

readily available for examination.[24] Not documenting the review and approval of financial management information increases the risk that these procedures may not be performed effectively and that as a result significant errors may not be prevented or be detected and corrected in a timely manner, adversely affecting the reliability of the information provided to key stakeholders.

Conclusions

In order to make informed decisions regarding matters affecting the financial aspects of operations and the performance of programs, it is critical that decision makers have available timely and reliable information. This is particularly true as it relates to programs that have been subject to the significant degree of public and congressional scrutiny that has characterized the implementation of PPACA, including the CCIIO-related private health insurance and health insurance exchange provisions. However, CMS does not have documented policies and procedures governing responses to nonroutine information requests, such as those that may originate from oversight bodies. CMS's reliance on manual procedures and personal recollection resulted in an inefficient and time-consuming process to provide the requested information. In addition, because of the manner in which CMS accounts for and retains CCIIO-related financial management information, we could not determine the reliability of most of it. Also, because its process for obtaining the information and its review and approval of the information provided were not documented, there is no assurance that such procedures have been properly performed. Collectively, these issues increase the risk that significant errors may not be prevented or detected and corrected before information is provided in response to requests from Congress and other decision makers. Consequently, such users of these data may not have timely and reliable CCIIIO-related financial management information, which could hamper their efforts to make informed resource allocation decisions and assessments of program performance.

Recommendations for Executive Action

We recommend that the Secretary of Health and Human Services direct the Administrator of the Centers for Medicare and Medicaid Services to take the following actions:

---

[24]GAO/AIMD-00-21.3.1.

- identify and evaluate options to facilitate more timely and independently verifiable reporting of CCIIO-related financial management information, such as enhancing HIGLAS's standard reporting or custom reporting capabilities, and

- develop and implement policies and procedures for responding to nonroutine CCIIO-related financial management information requests, including procedures for documenting the preparation process and the review and approval of the results.

Agency Comments and Our Evaluation

We provided a draft of this report to HHS for comment. In its written comments, reprinted in appendix II, HHS did not concur with our two recommendations. HHS also provided technical comments, which we incorporated as appropriate.

HHS did not concur with our recommendation that it identify and evaluate options to facilitate more timely and independently verifiable reporting of CCIIO-related financial management information, such as enhancing HIGLAS's standard reporting or custom reporting capabilities. HHS indicated that in response to our requests, it gave us supporting data to permit validation and verification of the information it provided, including numerous summary tables and detailed transaction-level reports from HIGLAS. We disagree with HHS's response. As discussed in our report, CMS was able to provide us with CCIIO-related obligation and expenditure amounts from appropriation accounts that exclusively funded CCIIO-related activities. For these accounts, we were able to assess completeness by comparing the amounts provided to summary totals in HIGLAS. However, for appropriation accounts that funded both CCIIO-related and non-CCIIO-related activities, CMS utilized a time-consuming manual process to extract the obligation and expenditure activity from HIGLAS, and the accounting code structure did not allow CMS to provide related HIGLAS summary totals. Without the ability to compare the information provided by CMS for all accounts with CCIIO-related activity to summary totals in HIGLAS, we were unable to determine that the total amounts of CCIIO-related obligations and expenditures CMS provided were complete, which is a major factor in determining reliability.

HHS also indicated that we could have determined the reliability of CCIIO-related obligations and expenditures by using the same procedures we used to determine that CMS's estimates of CCIIO-related total obligations for expenditures for fiscal year 2014 were reliable. However, we were able to verify the reliability of obligation estimates for fiscal year 2014 using budget data because estimates of future activity are not supported by past (actual) transaction activity. Therefore, our ability to verify these estimates was not affected by the lack of associated HIGLAS totals which affected our ability to verify the reliability of actual obligation and expenditure data for fiscal years 2010 through 2013. As discussed in our report, Statement of Federal Financial Accounting Standards No. 4, *Managerial Cost Accounting Standards and Concepts*, and Statement of Federal Financial Accounting Concepts No.1, *Objectives of Federal Financial Reporting*, highlight the importance of providing reliable and timely information to key stakeholders, including Congress, to support informed resource allocation decisions and assessments of program performance, and the need for such information to be verifiable. As discussed in our report, CMS sometimes took months to provide the information we requested and did not always provide CCIIO-related information whose reliability could be independently determined, thereby limiting the type and usefulness of information available to Congress and other decision makers for making informed decisions. HHS concluded its response with a statement that it will continue to evaluate options for enhancing HIGLAS's "standard reporting and/or custom reporting capabilities." We continue to believe that identifying and considering such options will help facilitate the timely response to stakeholder requests for reliable information on HHS programs, particularly for programs subject to a significant degree of public and congressional scrutiny.

HHS also did not agree with our recommendation that it develop and implement policies and procedures for responding to nonroutine CCIIO-related financial management information requests, including procedures for documenting the preparation process and the review and approval of the results. In its response, HHS stated that it has up-to-date and clearly documented standard operating procedures (SOP) for its normal day-to-day work processes and employs ad hoc teams and processes to address data requests for information that differs from HIGLAS standard reports. HHS also stated that the varying nature of data requests for nonroutine reports does not easily lend itself to utilizing one documented SOP. We agree that it would be difficult to develop an individual SOP for each specific CCIIO-related data request, but we continue to believe that regardless of the specifics of each request, common processes and controls that are necessary should be documented and required in written policies and procedures. For example, as discussed in the report, CMS did not have a policy or procedures that required documented review and approval of the information provided in response to nonroutine requests. Such documented review and approval would help ensure the reliability of the information CMS provided, regardless of the specific data request. Although HHS stated that subject matter experts were involved in all steps of identifying a methodology, extracting data from multiple systems, and manually producing reports in order to meet the requests for customized displays of information and that it conducted multiple levels of review prior to providing the information, none of these steps or reviews were documented, as noted in our report. As a result, we were not able to independently verify that these steps and reviews actually took place. Similarly, absent documented review and approval, management lacks assurance that these important controls are in place, increasing the risk that errors may not be prevented or detected and corrected in a timely manner.

We are sending copies of this report to appropriate congressional committees, the Secretary of Health and Human Services, the Administrator of the Centers for Medicare and Medicaid Services, the Director of the Office of Management and Budget, and other interested parties. In addition, the report is available at no charge on the GAO website at http://www.gao.gov.

If you or your staff have any questions about this report, please contact me at (202) 512-2623 or davisbh@gao.gov. Contact points for our Offices of Congressional Relations and Public Affairs may be found on the last page of this report. GAO staff who made key contributions to this report are listed in appendix III.

Beryl H. Davis
Director
Financial Management and Assurance

Appendix I: Objective, Scope, and Methodology

Our objective was to identify the resources related to the Center for Consumer Information and Insurance Oversight (CCIIO) that the Centers for Medicare and Medicaid Services (CMS) received, used, and expects to use from enactment of the Patient Protection and Affordable Care Act (PPACA) though fiscal year 2014, including certain categories of expenditures; the source of the funding; the number of CCIIO staff as of September 30, 2013; and the number of staff reassigned from other units. The scope of our review encompassed the financial and staff resources provided to and used by CMS to help implement the private health insurance and health insurance exchange provisions of PPACA from enactment in March 2010 through fiscal year 2013 and the amounts CMS estimates it will use for fiscal year 2014.

To achieve our audit objective, we contacted responsible officials at CMS to request the (1) data concerning total CCIIO-related obligations and expenditures[1] from the enactment of PPACA in March 2010 through fiscal year 2013, including amounts related to salaries, travel, advertising and other public relations activities, polling and focus groups, and conferences; (2) CMS's estimates of obligations in total and in each of these categories for fiscal year 2014; and (3) the number of full- and part-time CCIIO staff as of September 30, 2013, including the number reassigned from other CMS and Department of Health and Human Services (HHS) units. We also requested available supporting documentation for the information requested to assist in determining its reliability. We reviewed policies and procedures—including internal controls in place to ensure the reliability of the information CMS provided—in order to assess the information's applicability to our audit objectives and its conformance with internal control standards.[2] In order to determine whether the information CMS provided was reliable,[3] we

---

[1]Obligations are legal liabilities of an agency to pay for goods and services ordered or received. An agency incurs an obligation, for example, when it places an order, signs a contract, awards a grant, purchases a service, or takes other actions that require the government to make payments to the public or from one government account to another. Expenditures are the actual spending of money through the issuance of checks, disbursement of cash, or electronic transfer of funds made to liquidate an obligation.

[2]GAO, *Standards for Internal Control in the Federal Government*, GAO/AIMD-00-21.3.1 (Washington, D.C.: November 1999).

[3]For financial information to be considered reliable, it must be determined to be (1) complete (includes all applicable information), (2) accurate (free of material error or fraud), and (3) valid (includes only financial information that accurately represents the substance of the nature of the underlying financial activity).

analyzed the information we received, conducted extensive follow-up inquiries with agency officials to ensure that we had received what we requested, and compared the information to available supporting documentation. Specifically, we

- compared the detailed financial information CMS extracted from the Healthcare Integrated General Ledger Accounting System (HIGLAS) to its related totals, where available, to determine whether all appropriate information had been extracted and the amounts provided by CMS were complete and

- estimated the amount of salaries based on detailed information on individual grade levels and pay rates that CMS obtained from its payroll system and compared the amount to the total salaries CMS obtained from HIGLAS to determine whether the total number of employees and related staff salary data were reliable as of September 30, 2013.

To determine the reasonableness of CCIIO's estimated funding and spending amounts for fiscal year 2014, we compared CMS's estimates to the President's budget, with the exception of changes made subsequent to preparation of the President's budget.[4] For such changes to the estimates, we obtained an understanding of the basis upon which the changes were developed to determine if they were reasonable.

As described in our report, we could not determine the reliability of most of the data provided to us. We also met with officials from the Office of Inspector General of HHS and CMS's independent financial statement auditor to determine whether they were aware of any internal control or substantive issues pertinent to CCIIO-related activities that could affect our ability to rely upon the financial management information CMS provided.

---

[4]Office of Management and Budget, *Fiscal Year 2014 Budget of the U.S. Government* (Washington, D.C.: Apr. 10, 2013).

Appendix II: Comments from the Department of Health and Human Services

DEPARTMENT OF HEALTH & HUMAN SERVICES

OFFICE OF THE SECRETARY

Assistant Secretary for Legislation
Washington, DC 20201

SEP 5 2014

Beryl H. Davis
Director, Financial Management and Assurance
U.S. Government Accountability Office
441 G Street NW
Washington, DC 20548

Dear Mr. Davis:

Attached are comments on the U.S. Government Accountability Office's (GAO) correspondence entitled, "Patient Protection and Affordable Care Act: Procedures for Reporting Certain Financial Management Information Should Be Improved" (GAO-14-697).

The Department appreciates the opportunity to review this report prior to publication.

Sincerely,

Jim R. Esquea
Assistant Secretary for Legislation

Attachment

<u>GENERAL COMMENTS OF THE DEPARTMENT OF HEALTH AND HUMAN
SERVICES (HHS) ON THE GOVERNMENT ACCOUNTABILITY OFFICE'S DRAFT
REPORT ENTITLED: PATIENT PROTECTION AND AFFORDABLE CARE ACT:
PROCEDURES FOR REPORTING CERTAIN FINANCIAL MANAGEMENT
INFORMATION SHOULD BE IMPROVED (GAO-14-697)</u>

The Department appreciates the opportunity to review and comment on this draft report.

Recommendation 1
Identify and evaluate options to facilitate more timely and independently verifiable reporting of
CCIIO-related financial management information, such as enhancing HIGLAS' standard
reporting or custom reporting capabilities.

HHS Response
HHS does not concur with this recommendation. HHS appropriately tracks appropriations in
accordance with all relevant Federal laws and regulations. The Federal accounting concepts and
standards around managerial cost accounting are broad and allow maximum flexibility for
agency managers to develop costing methods that are best suited to their operational
environment. HHS has worked with all its partners and stakeholders to develop an accounting
system that tracks funds appropriately.

CMS ensures efficient and effective operations and financial accountability by tracking
obligations and expenditures by specific accounts created by an appropriation, such as the
Consumer Operated and Oriented Plan Program; the Pre-Existing Condition Insurance Plan
Program; or the Early Retiree and Reinsurance Program within the accounting system. CMS
accounting and financial reporting processes are robust and in compliance with Statements of
Federal Financial Accounting Standards (SFFAS), and Office of Management and Budget
Circulars A-136 and A-11. As designed, The Healthcare Integrated General Ledger Accounting
System (HIGLAS) was programmed to comply with legislative and government-wide reporting
guidelines, and permits tracking of accounting transactions based on specific accounting code
structures.

During the GAO review, in response to specific requests for CCIIO-related obligations and
expenditures, HHS provided GAO with supporting information to permit validation and
verification of CMS' Center for Consumer Information and Insurance Oversight (OCCIIO)
related information, including numerous summary tables and detailed transaction level reports
from HIGLAS. We also met with GAO throughout the review to explain our methodology for
determining CMS' CCIIO-related transactions that included direct appropriations, appropriations
for general operations, and cost allocations methodologies. We believe the information provided
to GAO was complete and verifiable based upon the information and transactional level data that
was provided, consistent with published Operating Plans and the President's Budget. As stated
in this report, GAO employed this same verification technique to determine that CMS' estimates
of CCIIO-related total obligations for expenditures for fiscal year 2014 were reliable.

HHS will continue to evaluate options for enhancing HIGLAS' standard reporting and/or custom
reporting capabilities, with the immediate focus to ensure the success of the HIGLAS technical
upgrade (approved in June 2014) to Oracle Release 12.

<u>**Recommendation 2**</u>
Develop and implement policies and procedures for responding to non-routine CCIIO related financial management information requests, including procedures for documenting the preparation process and the review and approval of the results.

<u>**HHS Response**</u>
HHS does not concur with this recommendation. HHS has up-to-date and clearly documented standard operating procedures (SOPs) for its normal day-to-day work processes. HHS employees rely on written SOPs to complete their day-to-day activities to ensure there are proper internal controls. These SOPs are also documented and routinely updated in cycle memos that are reviewed and/or audited under OMB Circular A-123 and the CFO Audit. HHS uses standard processes to the maximum extent possible for standard information required for government-wide reporting, and employs ad hoc teams and processes to address data requests for information that differs from HIGLAS standard reports. The varying nature of data requests for non-routine reports does not easily lend itself to utilizing one documented SOP. Instead, HHS carefully evaluates each unique request to provide accurate information.

Throughout the engagement, HHS clarified our methodology for determining which obligations and expenditures were deemed "CCIIO- related." Subject matter experts were involved in all steps of identifying a methodology, extracting data from multiple systems, and manually producing reports in order to meet requests for customized displays of information. To ensure data accuracy, HHS conducted multiple levels of review prior to providing the information. HHS made every effort to comply with information requests, including meeting with GAO throughout the review to explain how data was compiled and providing detailed level support, including numerous tables and detailed transactional reports

Appendix III: GAO Contact and Staff Acknowledgments

GAO Contact	Beryl H. Davis, (202) 512-2623 or davisbh@gao.gov
Staff Acknowledgments	In addition to the contact named above, Charles Fox (Assistant Director), William Brown, Joshua Edelman, Wilfred Holloway, Robert Mabasa, Phillip McIntyre, and John Warner made key contributions to this report.